AMERICA'S MOST WINNING TEAMS™

NEBRASKA FOOTBALL

CARLA MOONEY

rosen publishing's
rosen central®

New York

Published in 2014 by The Rosen Publishing Group, Inc.
29 East 21st Street, New York, NY 10010

Library of Congress Cataloging-in-Publication Data

Mooney, Carla, 1970-.
Nebraska football/Carla Mooney.—1st ed.—New York: Rosen, c2014
    p. cm.—(America's most winning teams)
Includes bibliographical references and index.
ISBN: 978-1-4488-9400-0 (Library Binding)
ISBN: 978-1-4488-9433-8 (Paperback)
ISBN: 978-1-4488-9434-5 (6-pack)
1. Football—History—Juvenile literature. 2. Nebraska Cornhuskers (Football team)—Juvenile literature. 3. University of Nebraska—Lincoln—Football—History—Juvenile literature. 4. Nebraska Cornhuskers (Football team)—History.
I. Title.
GV958.U53 .M66 2014
796.332

Manufactured in the United States of America

CPSIA Compliance Information: Batch #S13YA: For further information, contact Rosen Publishing, New York, New York, at 1-800-237-9932.

CONTENTS

INTRODUCTION

Over the past century, the Nebraska Cornhuskers have been one of the country's most winning college football programs. The Cornhuskers represent the University of Nebraska in Lincoln, Nebraska. Over the years, the Cornhuskers have generated impressive numbers. They have been crowned national champions five times. They have won forty-three conference championships. Eleven times, the Nebraska football team has gone undefeated for an entire season. Nebraska is one of only eleven football programs in NCAA (National Collegiate Athletic Association) Division I-A history to win eight hundred or more games.

Many standout players have worn Nebraska's red and white uniforms. Three Cornhuskers have won college football's prestigious Heisman Trophy Award, given to the best college football player each year. Dozens of Cornhuskers have earned all-American honors. These players have had their names recorded in Cornhusker, conference, and NCAA record books.

Still, the magic of the Nebraska Cornhuskers cannot be told simply by impressive numbers and statistics alone. On Saturday game days, Nebraska's Memorial Stadium rocks in red

A rainbow rises over the crowd of Husker fans at Nebraska's Memorial Stadium during a Cornhuskers game against the rival Oklahoma Sooners. The stadium was dedicated in 1923.

and white as fans cheer for their beloved Huskers. Tradition and pageantry fill the stadium as the Huskers take the field. For players, students, alumni, and fans, Nebraska football is more than a game. In the words of Nebraska alumni and former ESPN commentator Trev Alberts, "It was pretty clear that Nebraska football wasn't just a game and not even a passion, but rather a way of life."

CHAPTER 1

HUSKER HISTORY

On Thanksgiving Day, November 27, 1890, the football team from the University of Nebraska suited up to play their first game. As fans waved banners of gold, the Nebraska team defeated the Omaha YMCA, 10–0. That game, played more than a century ago, marked the beginning of Nebraska's rich football tradition.

THE EARLY YEARS

In its first season in 1890, Nebraska played only one other game. The team also defeated Doane College in Crete, Nebraska. Over the next few years, Nebraska added new opponents outside the state, including Iowa and Illinois. The early football program started Nebraska's winning tradition. The team had only one losing season in its first twenty-eight years.

During the early years, several team traditions emerged. In 1892, the school changed its colors from gold to scarlet red and cream. The team also had a number of nicknames. Fans called them Bugeaters, Tree-planters, Rattlesnake Boys, Antelopes, and the Old Gold Knights. In 1899, a newspaper began calling the team the Cornhuskers. The nickname stuck and became the team and school's official nickname in 1900.

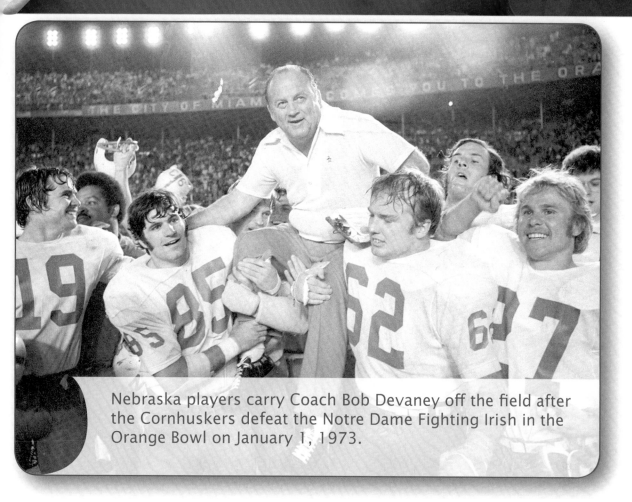

Nebraska players carry Coach Bob Devaney off the field after the Cornhuskers defeat the Notre Dame Fighting Irish in the Orange Bowl on January 1, 1973.

From 1894 through 1937, the Cornhuskers played in three conferences: the Western Inter-State Conference Association, the Missouri Valley Conference, and the Big Eight Conference. During this time, Nebraska dominated many opponents and won twenty-three conference championships. As the nation struggled through the Great Depression of the 1930s, Nebraskans took pride in the success of the Cornhusker football team.

In the 1940 season, the Cornhuskers accepted an invitation to play in the Rose Bowl in California on January 1, 1941. It was the first bowl bid for the Cornhuskers. Fans celebrated the invitation for twenty-four hours after hearing the news, singing the school song, "There Is No Place Like Nebraska."

Although the Cornhuskers lost the Rose Bowl to Stanford, bowl games have since become a regular occurrence for Nebraska football. From 1969 to 2003, the Cornhuskers made thirty-five consecutive bowl trips, an NCAA record.

HOME OF THE HUSKERS: MEMORIAL STADIUM

From 1909 through 1923, the Cornhuskers played home games at Nebraska Athletic Field. The field held about 10,000 fans. As Nebraska football's popularity grew, the field became too small. A new stadium was built during 1922. It was named Memorial Stadium in honor of Nebraska veterans who fought in World War I, the Spanish-American War, and the Civil War.

On October 23, 1923, Nebraska dedicated the new football stadium. The new stadium held about 31,000 fans. This was three times the amount that the old Nebraska Athletic Field held. Since 1923, Memorial Stadium has been the home of Nebraska football. Since it first opened in 1923, Memorial Stadium has undergone several expansions. Today, the stadium holds more than 80,000 fans at each home game.

WAR YEARS SLUMP

In the late 1930s and early 1940s, the world's attention was focused on World War II. Many young men volunteered to serve in America's armed forces. As a result, few strong, young men were available to play college football.

Football at Nebraska slumped during the war years. Beginning in 1941, the Cornhuskers fell into a slump that lasted through 1961. During this time, the Huskers had a series of coaches and several losing seasons.

MASCOTS: HERBIE HUSKER AND LIL' RED

Herbie Husker became the Cornhusker mascot following the 1974 Cotton Bowl. He was based on a cartoon character created by Texas artist Dirk West. When Nebraska sports information director Don Bryant saw West's cartoon, he hired West to design the Cornhusker mascot. In 2005, Herbie Husker was named the National Mascot of the Year.

In 1994, Lil' Red joined Herbie Husker as a Nebraska mascot. Lil' Red is one of the first sports mascot inflatable characters. A crowd favorite, Lil' Red is known for dancing on the sidelines during Husker football games.

Nebraska's well-known mascot Herbie Husker waves a Nebraska flag as he cheers for the Cornhuskers during a game against the Ohio State Buckeyes.

NEBRASKA DYNASTY DOMINATES

In 1962, Nebraska hired a new head football coach, Bob Devaney. Under his leadership, a Cornhusker football dynasty began. Devaney turned the football program around immediately. During his first five seasons, the Huskers had a record of 47–8–0. They appeared in five bowl games. In 1969, the Cornhuskers began a thirty-two-game unbeaten streak that did not end until the first game of the 1972 season.

In 1970, Devaney led the Cornhuskers to their first national championship. The following year, the Cornhuskers repeated as national champions. In fact, the 1971 Cornhusker team is considered one of the best in college football history. By the time Devaney retired in 1972, Nebraska was a nationally recognized powerhouse.

During this time, many Cornhusker players earned national recognition. Eighteen players earned all-American honors. Cornhusker Johnny Rodgers won the Heisman Trophy in 1972. Defensive player Rich Glover won the Outland Trophy and Lombardi Award that same year.

After Devaney's retirement, Tom Osborne became Nebraska's head football coach. Under Osborne, the Nebraska dynasty continued. The Cornhuskers won or shared thirteen conference championships between 1973 and 1997. They also won three more national championships in 1994, 1995, and 1997.

HUSKERS TODAY

Over the years, Nebraska has played in several conferences, including the Western Inter-State Conference Association,

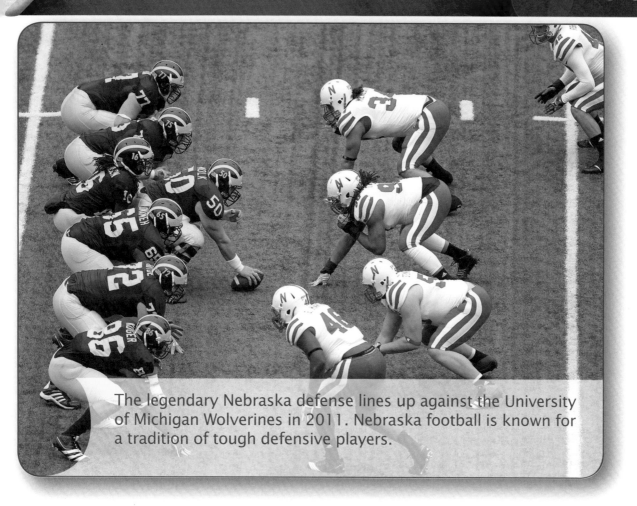

The legendary Nebraska defense lines up against the University of Michigan Wolverines in 2011. Nebraska football is known for a tradition of tough defensive players.

the Missouri Valley Conference, the Big Six Conference, the Big Eight Conference, and the Big 12 Conference. During this time, Nebraska has won or shared forty-three conference championships. In 2011, the Cornhuskers joined the Big Ten conference. Current Nebraska head coach Bo Pelini has guided the Huskers since 2008. Under his leadership, the Huskers have had a winning record every year through the 2012 season.

With more than 120 years of football and 1,200 games played, the Nebraska Cornhuskers have a long and proud football history. While embracing past traditions, the Cornhuskers are also looking forward to more success in the future.

CHAPTER 2

LEGENDARY COACHES

Several men who have led Nebraska's football team have become legendary figures in college football history. In recognition of their achievements, six Cornhusker coaches have been inducted into the College Football Hall of Fame.

THE EARLY YEARS

Several coaches shared in Nebraska's early success. Eddie "Robbie" Robinson (1896–1897) and Fielding Yost (1898) spent only a short time at Nebraska. They were the first Nebraska coaches to be inducted into the College Football Hall of Fame. Although Coach Ewald Stiehm (1911–1915) is not a Hall of Famer, he won the conference title in each of his five seasons with the Cornhuskers. He had a winning percentage of 0.913. This is still the best winning percentage of any Nebraska head coach.

In 1929, Dana Bible (1929–1936) took over as the Cornhusker head coach. He had fifteen years of experience, leading Texas A&M to five Southwest Conference titles. Coach Bible led Nebraska to six conference titles in eight seasons. In 1951, Bible was inducted into the College Football Hall of Fame.

Following Bible, Lawrence McCeney "Biff" Jones (1937–1941) became the Huskers' head coach. Although

Coach Dana Bible talks to players during a game. Coach Bible led the Cornhuskers from 1929 to 1936. Under him, the Cornhuskers won six conference titles in eight seasons.

not as successful as some of the previous Nebraska coaches, Jones led Nebraska to two conference titles. He also led the team to its first bowl game, the 1941 Rose Bowl. Jones was inducted into the College Football Hall of Fame in 1954.

Following Jones, America's attention turned to World War II. The country entered the war in 1942, after the bombing of Pearl Harbor. Thousands of young men joined the armed forces. During this time, Nebraska football declined. Several coaches led mediocre teams, and the Cornhuskers had several losing seasons. This downturn lasted until 1961, when Bob Devaney, one of Nebraska's most famous head coaches, was hired.

BOB DEVANEY (1962–1972)

After the 1961 season, Nebraska officials searched for a new football head coach. At first, they asked Michigan State's Duffy Daugherty. Daugherty turned down the job, but he recommended a former assistant, Bob Devaney. Devaney was then coaching Wyoming. After interviewing, Devaney was hired. Almost immediately, he turned the Nebraska program around and posted a 9–2 winning season in his first year.

During his eleven seasons as head football coach, Devaney's teams won 101 games. This gave him a remarkable 0.829 winning percentage. Under Devaney's guidance, the Cornhuskers won eight conference championships. They played in nine bowl games. Moreover, for the first time in Nebraska history, the Cornhuskers won the national championship in 1970. Their outright dominance continued in 1971, and Devaney led the Huskers to a second national championship. In 1972, Devaney attempted to lead the Huskers to an unprecedented third straight national championship. However, the team fell short and finished fourth

Bob Devaney coached the Cornhuskers for eleven seasons and led them to two national championships, in 1970 and 1972. He remains one of college football's most winning coaches.

TUNNEL WALK TRADITION

The Tunnel Walk tradition at Nebraska home games began in 1994. Before each game at Memorial Stadium, Husker fans watch on large video screens as the football players leave the locker room while stadium speakers play the Alan Parsons Project's instrumental "Sirius." The cameras follow the players as they walk down a hallway and through a tunnel that emerges beneath the stadium stands. The players raise their hands to touch a lucky horseshoe that hangs above the door as they leave the tunnel. They burst onto the field through the Tunnel Walk gates to the frenzied roar of Cornhusker fans.

in the nation. When he retired in 1973, Devaney was the country's most winning active coach. Today he is eleventh on the all-time list of winning coaches.

After football, Devaney remained involved in Nebraska athletics. He served as the school's athletic director from 1967 to 1993, and the athletic director emeritus from 1993 to 1996. Devaney retired in 1996. He remained in Lincoln, Nebraska, until he passed away at the age of eighty-two in 1997. His thirty-five-year success with the football program and the athletic department has made him one of the greatest Nebraska legends of all time.

TOM OSBORNE (1973–1997)

Following a coaching legend is a difficult job, but Tom Osborne was handpicked by Coach Devaney himself. During Devaney's national championship seasons, Osborne was a young assistant coach. He called the offensive plays from the coaches' box. When Devaney retired, he picked Osborne to lead the football team. Devaney announced the decision before the 1972 season.

Osborne was a Nebraskan and a multisport athlete. He had played professional football briefly. Yet he never planned to become a football coach. In fact, Osborne was hired on Devaney's staff while he was working on a post-graduate degree in educational psychology. The assistant coaching job offered free room and board, so Osborne accepted.

By the time he finished his doctorate degree, Osborne decided to keep coaching instead of teaching in a classroom.

Nebraska players prepare to dump a bucket of water on head coach Tom Osborne to celebrate a Cornhusker victory. Coach Osborne led the Cornhuskers to three national championships.

After he became Nebraska's head coach, Osborne led the football team for twenty-five years, the most years for any Nebraska football coach.

Under his guidance, the Cornhuskers achieved remarkable success. Osborne's teams won at least nine games every year. Osborne's winning percentage of 0.836 makes him the fifth all-time winning coach in Division 1 history. Osborne's teams played in twenty-five consecutive bowl games, an NCAA coaching record. His teams won or shared thirteen conference titles. Osborne also led Nebraska to back-to-back national championships in 1994 and 1995. The 1994 and 1995 teams were undefeated, making Nebraska only the second school in history to have back-to-back perfect national championship seasons. In 1997, Osborne's Cornhuskers shared the national title with Michigan. During Osborne's last five years of coaching, his Nebraska teams had an incredible 60–3 record, the best five-year record in

At a home game, the Nebraska fans displayed a special thank-you message to former coach Tom Osborne when he retired as Nebraska's athletic director in 2012.

college football history. After his third national champion-ship, Osborne retired for health and personal reasons.

Off the field, Osborne achieved success as well. He dedi-cated himself to developing well-rounded student-athletes. His players earned sixty-five Academic All-American awards dur-ing his twenty-five years as football coach. In fact, Osborne produced more Academic All-Americans at Nebraska than any other football program has produced in its history.

After coaching, Osborne turned to politics. He was elected to the U.S. House of Representatives in 2000, 2002, and 2004. He ran for Nebraska governor in 2006, but lost to incumbent Dave Heineman in the Republican primary.

In 2007, Osborne returned to Nebraska athletics as ath-letic director. He hired the current football coach, Bo Pelini, who has brought new success to the Cornhusker program. Osborne was also instrumental in the school's move from the Big 12 conference to the Big Ten in 2011. He guided new building projects and expanded Memorial Stadium to hold more than 90,000 fans. In the fall of 2012, Osborne announced that he would be retiring as athletic director after the 2012 football season.

In recognition of his achievements, Nebraska named the field at Memorial Stadium in honor of Osborne. In addition, the College Football Hall of Fame waved its man-datory three-year waiting period to induct Osborne in 1999. Osborne is one of only four coaches who have had the Hall of Fame's waiting period waived.

Together Bob Devaney and Tom Osborne are responsible for much of Nebraska's winning history. These Hall of Fame coaches each won more than one hundred games in back-to-back careers at Nebraska, the first major college coaching pair to do so at the same school.

CHAPTER 3

KEY RIVALRIES

Some of the most memorable games in Nebraska football history have been played against great rivals. Playing tough rivals has helped Nebraska become a better football team and has given fans some of their fondest memories.

EARLY RIVALS

Rivals of Nebraska's early teams included Notre Dame, Iowa, Minnesota, and Pittsburgh. Nebraska first played Notre Dame in 1915. The Cornhuskers won the game, 20–19. For the next ten years, the two teams faced each other annually. The matchup was fairly even, with each team winning five games and one game ending in a tie. Since 1925, the two teams have played less frequently. In 1973, they faced each other in the Orange Bowl. The Cornhuskers defeated Notre Dame, 40–6.

Nebraska's early rivalry with Iowa began because the two teams were geographically close to each other. The first game was played in 1891, Nebraska's second season. The two teams played regularly through 1946. Since then, the Cornhuskers and Hawkeyes have faced each other only six times.

In the early 1900s, Nebraska measured itself against football powerhouses Minnesota and Pittsburgh. Victories against these rivals were hard fought and rare. Winning against these rivals was something to

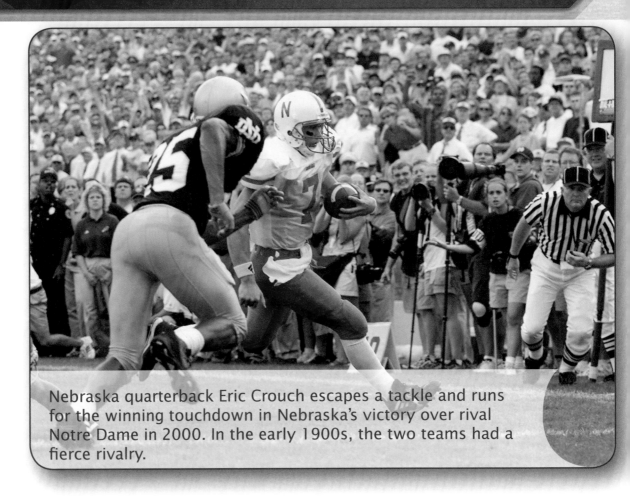

Nebraska quarterback Eric Crouch escapes a tackle and runs for the winning touchdown in Nebraska's victory over rival Notre Dame in 2000. In the early 1900s, the two teams had a fierce rivalry.

celebrate in Nebraska. Both rivalries faded over time as the teams met only a few times in recent decades.

KANSAS JAYHAWKS

Nebraska played Kansas for the first time in 1892. From 1906 through 2010, the two teams played each other every year. Their 105-year series became the longest continuous series in Division 1-A football. The results were often lopsided in Nebraska's favor. Fron 1917 to 1943, Nebraska did not lose a game to Kansas. From 1969 to 2004, they won thirty-six straight games against the Jayhawks. Overall, Nebraska holds a 91–23–3 record against Kansas.

A Nebraska wide receiver catches the ball and escapes a tackle by a KU player in a game at Memorial Stadium against the rival Kansas Jayhawks.

MISSOURI TIGERS

Since 1892, the Missouri Tigers and the Nebraska Cornhuskers have met 104 times through the 2011 season. Over the years, the Nebraska-Missouri rivalry has been fiercely competitive. In the early years, Nebraska dominated the series. They lost only six of the first thirty-one games played. In the 1940s and 1950s, Missouri won more frequently. By 1978, the series between the two teams was almost even, with Nebraska leading by only five games.

In 1978, the Tigers spoiled the Cornhuskers' championship dreams. The Cornhuskers were ranked number two in the nation. They hoped to win another national championship. In the final game of the regular season, Missouri beat the Huskers and dashed their hopes for another title. After that game, Nebraska launched a winning streak against Missouri. They would not lose another game to the Tigers until 2003.

At each Missouri-Nebraska game, the winner is awarded the Victory Bell. The tradition began in 1892, when members of two Nebraska fraternities took a church bell. They used the bell in annual contests. In 1926, it was suggested that an annual award be given for the Missouri-Nebraska football game. The bell was offered as the prize. The letters "M" and "N" were engraved on either side of the bell. The scores from each game are also engraved on the bell. Because Nebraska defeated Missouri in their last meeting in 2010, the bell is currently at home in Nebraska's Memorial Stadium.

Historically, the Missouri-Nebraska rivalry was a fan favorite for both teams. Many record-setting crowds gathered to watch the two rivals play. In recent years, the rivalry has lost some of its intensity. In 2011, Nebraska joined the

TOUCHDOWN BALLOONS

One of most memorable Cornhusker traditions takes flight after the Huskers score their first touchdown at a home game. For decades, the sky above Memorial Stadium has filled with thousands of red and white balloons that are released after the first Husker touchdown. In 2012, university officials announced that the touchdown balloon tradition would be put on hold because of a nationwide helium shortage. Fans hope that the red and white balloons will soon fill the Nebraska sky again.

Big Ten Conference. The two teams will no longer play each season. One day, the teams may meet again in a bowl game.

OKLAHOMA SOONERS

Many Nebraska fans will point to one team as their fiercest rival: the Oklahoma Sooners. Over the years, Nebraska and Oklahoma have battled on the football field, often with a championship in the balance. One of the most memorable contests was the epic 1971 "Game of the Century," which Nebraska won 35–31. In 1958, Nebraska defeated Oklahoma and ended their seventy-four-game conference-winning streak. In 2000, the Sooners beat the number one ranked Huskers, 31–14.

The rivalry between the Cornhuskers and Sooners began in 1912. It developed over the years as the teams played each other annually in the Big Six, Big Seven, and Big Eight conferences. The success of each program intensified their football rivalry. Often, the result of the game they played

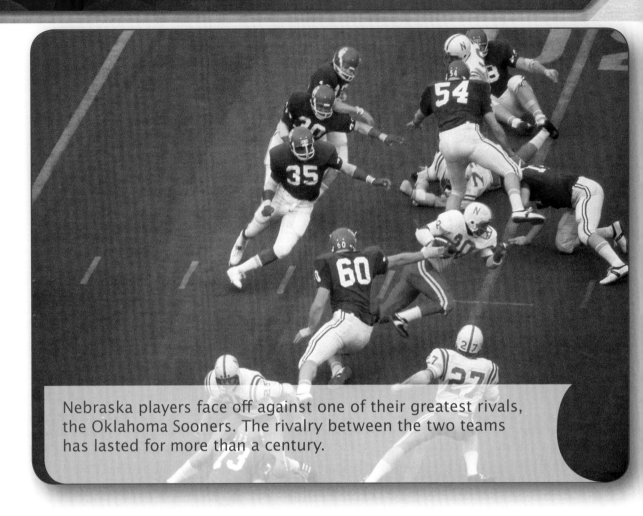

Nebraska players face off against one of their greatest rivals, the Oklahoma Sooners. The rivalry between the two teams has lasted for more than a century.

each year affected the conference championship. In the thirty-six seasons of the Big Eight, Nebraska or Oklahoma won or shared thirty-two of the championships.

Sometimes, the Nebraska-Oklahoma annual game affected the national championship. In the 1970s and 1980s, the teams played several games that decided the championship. During the 1970s, the two teams each won two national championships. Oklahoma may have won a third if they had not been upset by the Cornhuskers in 1978.

One of the most memorable games in Cornhusker history was played on Thanksgiving Day in 1971. It was called the Game of the Century. Coming into the matchup,

Nebraska was the number one–ranked team in the country and led the nation in defense. Oklahoma was ranked number two and led the country in offense. Both teams were undefeated. The winner would most likely be crowned national champion. The game proved to be as exciting as fans around the country anticipated. With a little more than seven minutes remaining, Oklahoma took the lead. In a defining drive, the Cornhusker offense drove 74 yards down the field. Legendary Cornhusker Johnny Rodgers caught a critical third-down pass to keep the drive alive. With 1:38 minutes remaining, the Huskers scored the go-ahead touchdown. They won the game, 35–31. The Cornhuskers finished the season undefeated and become national champions. Several years later in 1987, the Sooners would win a rematch called the Game of the Century II, 17–7.

The rivalry between Oklahoma and Nebraska continues today. In 1996, the formation of the Big 12 cut Nebraska-Oklahoma meetings down to two games every four years. Although they now do not play every year, the games between the rivals are as intense and hard fought as in years past. In 2000, Oklahoma knocked Nebraska from the number one ranking. The Cornhuskers did the same a year later, upsetting number two–ranked Oklahoma.

According to fans, the two rivals respect and appreciate each other. Their games have included some of the greatest players and coaches in college football history. No matter where or when, the Nebraska-Oklahoma game is sure to be an intense, hard-fought battle.

CHAPTER 4

STAR PLAYERS

Over the years, dozens of star players have worn Nebraska's red and white. Many of these young men won national awards. Some were voted into the College Football Hall of Fame. Three Nebraska players won the Heisman Trophy, an award given each year to the best college football player. In addition, many Nebraska players have been successful in the NFL, including defensive tackle Ndamukong Suh and wide receiver Irving Fryar.

TOM NOVAK (1946–1949)

Tom Novak anchored Nebraska's team in the late 1940s. He was one of the finest players in Nebraska history. His determination on the field earned him the nickname "Trainwreck." Novak was a two-way player. He lined up as a center on offense and a linebacker on defense. Novak earned all-conference honors every year from 1946

Tom "Trainwreck" Novak lunges for the ball. Novak was a key player for the Cornhuskers in the late 1940s. There is an award in his name, given to a top Nebraska senior each year.

through 1949. This made him Nebraska's only four-year all-conference player. He was also an all-American pick in 1949.

Although the Huskers had a losing record in the four seasons Novak played, he still shone as a star. More than sixty years later, his name remains in the Husker record books. Novak is tied for third on the all-time interception list (11). In addition, Novak still holds the single season interception record for linebackers (5). Norris Anderson, a sports editor for the *Lincoln Star* newspaper, wrote that no player ever gave more to Cornhusker football than Novak.

Immediately after his senior season, the team retired Novak's number 60 jersey. He was the first Husker to receive that honor. In 1950, the Huskers created the Tom Novak Award. Each year, the award is given to the Nebraska senior who best shows courage and determination. Years after his dominance on the field, Tom Novak passed away in 1998.

BOB BROWN (1961–1963)

According to legendary Husker coach Bob Devaney, Bob Brown was the best two-way player he ever coached. Brown played guard and linebacker for the Huskers in the early 1960s. Brown was also Nebraska's first African American to earn All-American honors.

Brown was an enormous player at the time. He lined up on the field at 6'5" (196 centimeters) and 260 pounds (118 kilograms). His dominance on the field helped Nebraska become one of the best football programs in the country. In 1963, Brown led Nebraska to its first Big Eight championship. Brown was inducted into the College Football Hall of Fame in 1993.

After graduating from Nebraska, Brown entered the 1964 NFL draft. The Philadelphia Eagles drafted him with the second pick. Over a ten-year career, Brown became one of the most feared offensive tackles in the NFL. He was selected to the Pro Bowl six times. He was also named to the NFL's All-Decade team for the 1960s. In 2004, Brown was voted into the Pro Football Hall of Fame. He is one of only three former Cornhuskers to earn the honor. In 2004, Nebraska retired Brown's number 64 jersey.

JOHNNY RODGERS (1970–1972)

Johnny "the Jet" Rodgers rocketed to stardom in the early 1970s. Rodgers played slot back and wide receiver. He also returned kicks with blazing style. His 72-yard punt return for a touchdown sparked the Huskers' thrilling win over Oklahoma in the 1971 Game of the Century. His 77-yard punt return touchdown also helped the Huskers defeat Alabama in the 1972 Orange Bowl, leading to their second national championship.

With the Huskers, Rodgers became the top pass receiver and kick returner in Big Eight history. He set forty-one Nebraska records and four NCAA records. He played for Cornhusker teams that were a combined 32–2–2 and won two national championships (1971 and 1972).

Rodgers won the Heisman Trophy in 1972. Then he ended his college career with an incredible game against Notre Dame in the 1973 Orange Bowl. He torched the Irish with 3 rushing touchdowns and a 50-yard touchdown reception. He even threw a touchdown pass in the Husker victory. In honor of his accomplishments, Rodgers was inducted into the College Football Hall of Fame in 2000.

MIKE ROZIER (1981–1983)

In the 1980s, Mike Rozier rushed his way into Nebraska legend and record books. Rozier's 4,780 career rushing yards

Johnny "the Jet" Rodgers electrified Nebraska fans with his blazing kick returns and fast play as receiver. Rodgers won the Heisman Trophy in 1972.

hold the record for both Nebraska and the Big Eight Conference. His 52 college touchdowns trail only fellow Heisman winner Eric Crouch.

During his first season, Rozier shared rushing duties with Rodger Craig. As a junior, Rozier stepped into the spotlight when Craig was injured. Rozier gained a Husker record 1,689 rushing yards in 1982. That year, he earned all-American and Big Eight Player of the Year honors. He also finished tenth in Heisman voting as a junior.

In his 1983 senior season, Rozier shattered the record books. He broke his own rushing records with 2,148 yards and 29 touchdowns. He became the second player in NCAA history to run for at least 2,000 yards in a single season. Rozier also broke Johnny Rodgers's 1972 record with 2,486 all-purpose

BLACKSHIRTS

The Blackshirts is a nickname for the Huskers' defense. It is also one of Nebraska's best-known football traditions. The Blackshirts began in the mid-1960s, when the NCAA allowed two-platoon football. This meant some players could now play only defense. Other players would play only offense.

At practice, coach Bob Devaney wanted an easy way to identify offensive and defensive players. He sent assistant coach Mike Corgan to a local sporting goods store to buy different colored jerseys for the defense. According to Nebraska legend, Corgan purchased black pullovers because they were a good deal.

Each day at practice, Devaney would hand out the black pullovers to first-team defenders. If a player did not practice well, he might not receive a black shirt the next day. Wearing the black shirts quickly became a source of pride for the defensive players.

Today, the Blackshirt jerseys have players' names and numbers. In recent years, coaches hand out the shirts the week before the opening game. The Blackshirts have become a symbol of the Husker defense.

yards. Rozier capped his senior season by winning several individual awards: his second all-American honor, the Heisman Trophy, the Maxwell Award, and the Walter Camp Player of the Year Award. He was voted into the College Football Hall of Fame in 2007.

TOMMIE FRAZIER (1992–1995)

Tommie Frazier earned his place as one of Nebraska's greatest players by playing his best in big games. Frazier quarter-backed the Huskers to back-to-back national championships in 1994 and 1995. During both title games, Frazier was named the most valuable player. During the 1994 season, Frazier had missed seven games because of a blood clot. He returned for the title game and led the Huskers to two fourth-quarter touch-downs. These scores propelled Nebraska to a 24–17 win over the Miami Hurricanes. The following year, Frazier rushed for 199 yards and 2 touchdowns in Nebraska's 62–24 win over Florida. His Huskers had won another national championship.

In 1995, Frazier became the first Husker to win the Johnny Unitas Golden Arm Award. He also finished second in voting for the Heisman Trophy and was a first-team All-American. Frazier still holds the school record of 43 passing touchdowns. He is second in the record books with 5,476 total offensive yards and 79 touchdowns. After leaving Nebraska, Frazier entered coaching. He is now the head coach at Doane College in Crete, Nebraska.

ERIC CROUCH (1998–2001)

Crouch rose to fame as one of the best option quarterbacks in college football history. When he finished his Nebraska career, Crouch was one of only three players in NCAA Division I-A

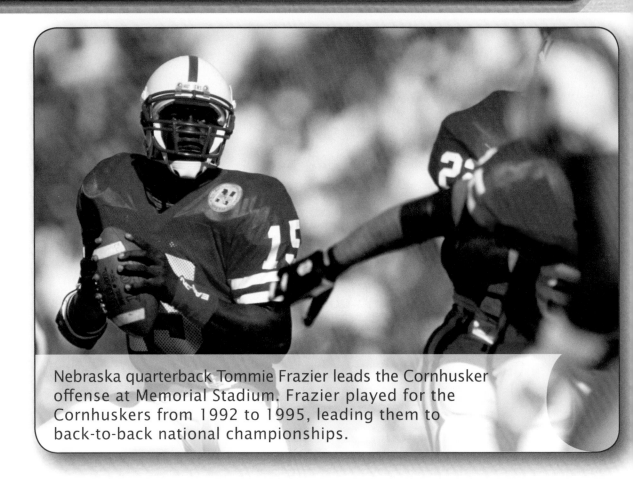

Nebraska quarterback Tommie Frazier leads the Cornhusker offense at Memorial Stadium. Frazier played for the Cornhuskers from 1992 to 1995, leading them to back-to-back national championships.

history to gain 3,000 yards rushing and 4,000 yards passing. He also scored 59 rushing touchdowns, an NCAA record for a quarterback.

During his 2001 senior season, Crouch led Nebraska to the Bowl Championship Series (BCS) title game against the Miami Hurricanes. During the championship game, Crouch rushed for 114 yards on the way to a Husker victory. For his outstanding play in 2001, Crouch won three individual honors: the Heisman Trophy, the Walter Camp Player of the Year Award, and the Davey O'Brien Quarterback Award.

At the end of his Nebraska career, Crouch held thirty-two school records. After he graduated in December 2001, the St. Louis Rams drafted Crouch as a wide receiver.

CHAPTER 5

CORNHUSKER CHAMPIONS

The Nebraska Cornhuskers have been champions throughout their history. The Cornhuskers have won or shared the coveted national championship title five times. They have been conference champions forty-three times. Nebraska has also been a perennial bowl invitee. They have played in bowl games more than forty times through the 2012 season.

DETERMINING A NATIONAL COLLEGE CHAMPION

Each week during the college football season, the top twenty-five teams in Division I-A are ranked by several organizations. The two most widely recognized rankings are the Associated Press (AP) poll and the coaches poll. The AP poll is a ranking of the teams by sportswriters across the country. The coaches poll reflects the rankings by the American Football Coaches Association's active coaches.

Until recent years, the NCAA did not hold a tournament or championship game to crown a college football national champion. Instead, most people declared the top-ranked team in the AP and coaches polls at the season's end as the championship winner. In some years when the polls disagreed on the number one team, this system resulted in two teams sharing the championship title. Beginning in 1988, the NCAA started the Bowl Championship Series (BCS) championship game. In this game, the number one–ranked and number two–ranked teams in the BCS mathematical ranking play each other. The winner is crowned the national champion.

1970 NATIONAL CHAMPIONSHIP

In 1970, there was no championship game played between the top two ranked college football teams. Instead, the

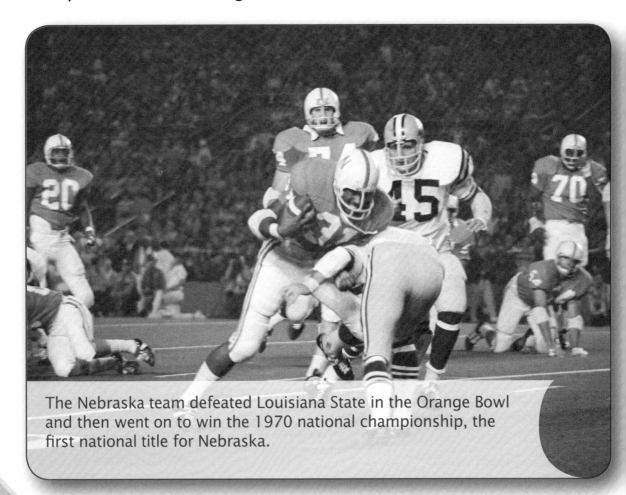

The Nebraska team defeated Louisiana State in the Orange Bowl and then went on to win the 1970 national championship, the first national title for Nebraska.

number one team in the AP and coaches polls was considered the national champion. Entering the Orange Bowl, Nebraska was ranked third in both the AP and coaches polls. Yet before the Cornhuskers kicked off their game, they learned that number one Texas had lost to Notre Dame in the Cotton Bowl and number two Ohio State had been beaten by Stanford in the Rose Bowl. The path to the national championship was now in Nebraska's hands.

In the Orange Bowl, the Cornhuskers prevailed over number five Louisiana State, 17–12. Although Notre Dame supporters called for their team to be ranked first, the Associated Press sportswriters voted overwhelmingly for the Nebraska Cornhuskers to take the top spot in the season-end rankings. Nebraska fans celebrated the first national championship in Husker history. The Huskers shared the title with Texas, who was voted number one in the coaches poll.

THE GREATEST TEAM: 1971 CHAMPIONS

Many consider the 1971 team to be the greatest in Husker history. Some say it may have been the greatest team in college football history. Coached by Bob Devaney, the team averaged more than 39 points a game. Their defense gave up an average of only 8.2 points per game. Nebraska faced stiff competition during the season from rival Big Eight teams, Oklahoma and Colorado. In fact, the final AP rankings put the three conference teams in the top three spots, a finish that has never been matched since.

The 1971 Cornhuskers featured many great players. All-Americans Johnny Rodgers (wingback), Jerry Tagge (quarterback), and Jeff Kinney (I-back) propelled the Husker

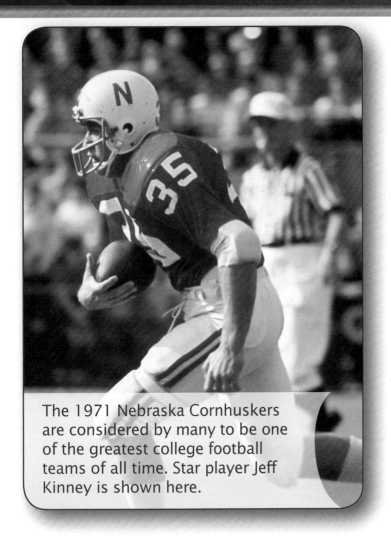

The 1971 Nebraska Cornhuskers are considered by many to be one of the greatest college football teams of all time. Star player Jeff Kinney is shown here.

offense. The Blackshirt defense was even more fearsome. Seven players were first-team, all-conference selections. The Nebraska defense ranked second in the country in rushing defense, third in scoring defense, and fifth in total defense. Three all-American players, Rich Glover, Willie Harper, and tackle Larry Jacobson, anchored the mighty Blackshirt defense.

On Thanksgiving Day 1971, number one Nebraska faced number two Oklahoma in the Game of the Century. Fans and players knew the game would likely decide which team would be the national champion. After a hard-fought battle, Nebraska defeated the Sooners 35–31.

In January, Nebraska defeated number two–ranked Alabama in the Orange Bowl. They outscored the Crimson Tide 38–6. Their dominant performance in the game and undefeated 13–0 season made them the top-ranked team in both the AP and coaches polls. They were the national champions for the second straight year.

THE RODGERS RETURN

In the 1971 Game of the Century, Johnny Rodgers made one of the most memorable plays in Cornhusker history. About four minutes into the game, Rodgers caught a punt from Oklahoma's Joe Wylie. With 61,000 fans watching in the stands and millions more watching on television, Rodgers raced 72 yards down the field for a touchdown, scoring the first points of the game. Known as the Rodgers Return, the key play is remembered by fans as one of the Nebraska football's greatest moments.

1994 NATIONAL CHAMPIONSHIP

In 1994, the Huskers were hungry for another national championship. The year before they had finished short, losing to Florida State in the Orange Bowl (18–16) on a missed field goal. Yet during the 1994 season, the Huskers and coach Tom Osborne faced more challenges. Several key players were injured. They lost safety Mike Minter for the season after a knee injury in the second game. Quarterback Tommie Frazier developed a blood-clot problem after the fourth game. When backup quarterback Brook Berringer's lung collapsed, walk-on player Matt Thurman had to start at quarterback against Kansas State.

Despite the challenges, Nebraska found a way to win. Berringer went 7–0 as the starting quarterback. The team won the Big Eight championship. They were invited to play in the Orange Bowl against the number three Miami Hurricanes. In the Orange Bowl, quarterback Frazier was cleared

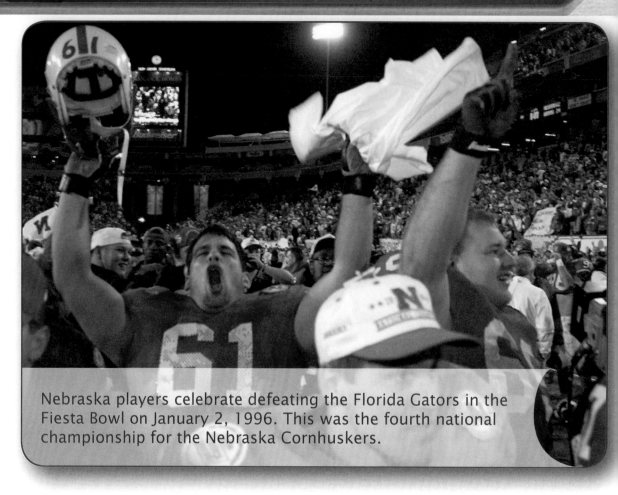

Nebraska players celebrate defeating the Florida Gators in the Fiesta Bowl on January 2, 1996. This was the fourth national championship for the Nebraska Cornhuskers.

to play. The Huskers were down 17–7 in the second half. They did not give up. The defense held the Hurricanes scoreless for the rest of the game and scored a safety. In the fourth quarter, the offense scored two touchdowns in less than five minutes to give the Huskers the victory, 24 to 17. The undefeated Huskers finished first in both the AP and coaches polls.

1995: BACK-TO-BACK CHAMPIONS

In 1995, Nebraska claimed its second consecutive championship. Coach Osborne's team rose to number one in the polls in late October. They did not give up the top spot for

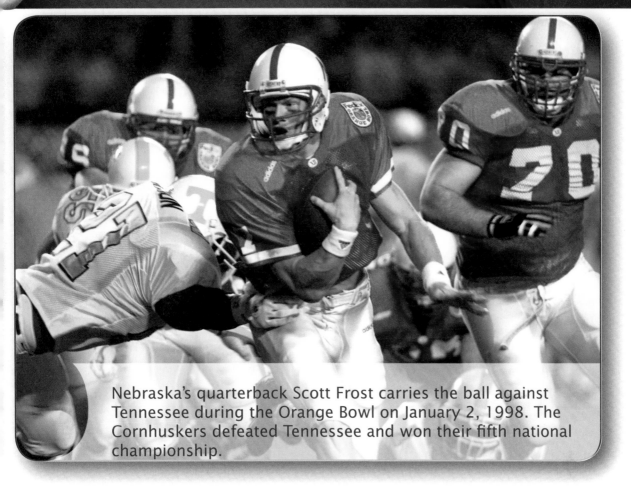

Nebraska's quarterback Scott Frost carries the ball against Tennessee during the Orange Bowl on January 2, 1998. The Cornhuskers defeated Tennessee and won their fifth national championship.

the rest of the season. The 1995 Cornhuskers had quarterback Tommie Frazier at the helm. He led the offense to lead the nation in rushing and scoring. The Husker offense also ranked second in total yards. At the Fiesta Bowl, the Cornhuskers overwhelmingly defeated the number two–ranked Florida Gators, 62–24. They finished first in both the AP and coaches polls. They had won their second back-to-back national championship.

1997 NATIONAL CHAMPIONS

In 1997, Nebraska won their third national title in four years. Ranked first by both polls in early November, the

Huskers survived a scare at Missouri. They pulled out an overtime victory, 45–38 over Missouri. After the game, the polls dropped Nebraska to number four and placed Michigan in the top spot. Nebraska kept fighting each week. They rose to the number two spot before their final game, the Orange Bowl.

Led by senior quarterback Scott Frost, Nebraska dominated a Tennessee team in the Orange Bowl. They won, 42–17. While Michigan also won their bowl game, it was a less impressive 21–16 victory over Washington State in the Rose Bowl. The door was open for the Huskers to take a piece of the national title. In the early morning hours, Husker players and fans celebrated when they learned that the national title had been split. The AP poll ranked Michigan first. The coaches poll placed Nebraska at the top. The Nebraska Cornhuskers shared the national championship, their fifth overall. With a long and rich championship history, the Nebraska Cornhuskers are one of America's most winning college football teams of all time.

1890: Nebraska plays its first football game against the Omaha YMCA, winning 10–0.

1892: Nebraska adopts scarlet red and cream as the school's colors.

1900: "Cornhuskers" becomes the official nickname of the Nebraska football team.

1911–1915: Coach Ewald Stiehm leads the Cornhuskers to five conference titles and a win percentage of 0.913.

1923: The university dedicates the new football stadium, Memorial Stadium.

1929: Coach Dana Bible takes over as head coach of the Cornhuskers and leads the team to six conference titles over the next eight seasons.

1937: Coach Biff Jones becomes the Husker head coach.

1941: On January 1, Nebraska plays in its first bowl game, the Rose Bowl.

1962: Nebraska hires head coach Bob Devaney.

1962: Nebraska begins its streak of selling out every home football game.

1970: Nebraska wins its first national championship, sharing the title with the Texas Longhorns.

1971: On Thanksgiving Day, Nebraska defeats rival Oklahoma in the Game of the Century. Nebraska wins its second national championship.

1972: Star player Johnny Rodgers wins the Heisman Trophy.

1973: Bob Devaney retires, and Tom Osborne becomes Nebraska's head coach.

1983: Running back Mike Rozier shatters records in his senior season and wins the Heisman Trophy.

1987: Rival Oklahoma defeats Nebraska in the Game of the Century II.

1994: Nebraska wins its third national championship.

1995: Nebraska wins its fourth national championship, its second back-to-back title.

1997: Nebraska wins its fifth national championship, sharing the title with Michigan.

1999: Coach Tom Osborne is inducted in the College Football Hall of Fame.

2001: Quarterback Eric Crouch wins the Heisman Trophy in his senior season.

2007: Tom Osborne returns as the Nebraska athletic director and hires current coach Bo Pelini for the 2008 season.

2011: Nebraska joins the Big Ten conference and continues the team's winning ways under head coach Bo Pelini.

GLOSSARY

all-American Selected as the best in the United States in a sport.

conference A league or an association of athletic teams.

consecutive Following one another without being interrupted.

dynasty A series of teams from the same school that are noted for their success.

expansion The enlargement of something, such as a building or stadium.

incumbent Currently holding an office or position.

inducted To be brought in as a member.

mascot An animal, person, or thing adopted by a group or team as its symbol or good luck charm.

mediocre Of ordinary quality, not very good or very bad.

option quarterback A quarterback who has the choice of running the ball if no receivers are open.

perennial Something that is continuing and recurring.

poll A sampling of opinions on a subject, such as the best college football team.

prestigious Having a high reputation and being honored.

ranking A list that shows the standing of each college football team in relation to other teams.

rival Another team that is competing for the same goal.

slump A decline in success, achieving less than before.

College Football Hall of Fame

111 South St. Joseph Street
South Bend, IN 466601
(800) 440-FAME (3263)
Web site: http://www.collegefootball.org
The College Football Hall of Fame honors and celebrates the best players
and coaches in college football.

Nebraska Alumni Association

1520 R Street
Lincoln, NE 68508-1651
(888) 353-1874
Web site: https://huskeralum.org
The Nebraska Alumni Association connects the University of Nebraska-
Lincoln with its students, alumni, and friends and provides informa-
tion about events, news, and features of interest to Nebraska fans.

University of Nebraska-Lincoln

1400 R Street
Lincoln, NE 68588
(402) 472-7211
Web site: http://www.unl.edu
The University of Nebraska-Lincoln is the home of the Nebraska Cornhusker football team and provides information about the university
and its athletic programs.

WEB SITES

Due to the changing nature of Internet links, Rosen Publishing has
developed an online list of Web sites related to the subject of this
book. This site is updated regularly. Please use this link to access
the list:

http://www.rosenlinks.com/AMWT/NEFB

FOR FURTHER READING

Babcock, Mike, and Rob Doster. *Game Day Nebraska Football: The Greatest Games, Players, Coaches and Teams in the Glorious Tradition of Cornhusker Football*. Chicago, IL: Triumph, 2006.

Corcoran, Mike. *The Game of the Century: Nebraska vs. Oklahoma in College Football's Ultimate Battle*. Lincoln, NE: University of Nebraska, 2004.

Doeden, Matt. *Play Football Like a Pro: Key Skills and Tips*. Mankato, MN: Capstone, 2011.

Frederick, Shane. *Football: The Math of the Game*. Mankato, MN: Capstone, 2012.

Gramling, Gary, Christina M. Tapper, and Paul Ulane. *1st and 10: Top 10 Lists of Everything Football*. New York, NY: Time Home Entertainment, 2011.

Jacobs, Greg, Kurt Dobler, and Beth L. Blair. *The Everything Kids' Football Book: The All-Time Greats, Legendary Teams, Today's Superstars—and Tips on Playing Like a Pro*. Avon, MA: Adams Media, 2010.

Monnig, Alex. *Nebraska Cornhuskers*. Minneapolis, MN: ABDO Publishing, 2013.

Monnig, Alex. *Oklahoma Sooners*. Minneapolis, MN: ABDO Publishing, 2013.

Osborne, Tom. *Beyond the Final Score: There's More to Life than the Game*. Ventura, CA: Regal, 2009.

Sommers, Michael. *Football in the Big 12*. New York, NY: Rosen Central, 2008.

Stewart, Mark, and Kent Stephens. *The Notre Dame Fighting Irish*. Chicago, IL: Norwood House, 2011.

BIBLIOGRAPHY

Babcock, Mike, and Rob Doster. *Game Day Nebraska Football: The Greatest Games, Players, Coaches and Teams in the Glorious Tradition of Cornhusker Football.* Chicago, IL: Triumph, 2006.

ESPN.com. "Best College Football Teams of All Time." Retrieved June 26, 2012 (http://espn.go.com/page2/s/list/colfootball /teams/best.html).

ESPN.com. "Tom Osborne to Retire." September 26, 2012. Retrieved October 25, 2012 (http://espn.go.com/college -sports/story/_/id/8427343/nebraska-cornhuskers-ad-tom -osborne-going-retire).

Huskerspot.com. "History of the Nebraska Cornhusker Football Team." Retrieved October 15, 2012 (http://www.huskerspot .com/history/nebraska-history-pt1.php).

Mascot Hall of Fame. "Herbie Husker and Lil Red." Retrieved October 15, 2012 (http://www.huskers.com/ViewArticle .dbml?DB_OEM_ID=100&ATCLID=204764889).

Mascot Hall of Fame. "Lil Red." Retrieved October 15, 2012 (http://www.mascothalloffame.com/virtual/hall/index.html ?staff_id=35).

McConnell, Luke. "Oklahoma-Nebraska: The End of a Historic Rivalry." Bleacher Report.com, July 4, 2010. Retrieved October 25, 2012 (http://bleacherreport.com/articles/415540-oklahoma -nebraska-the-end-of-a-historic-rivalry).

University of Nebraska–Lincoln. "Bob Devaney." Husker.com. Retrieved June 13, 2012 (http://www.huskers.com/ViewArticle .dbml?DB_OEM_ID=100&ATCLID=919762).

INDEX

ABOUT THE AUTHOR

Carla Mooney has a B.S. in economics from the University of Pennsylvania. She writes for young people and is the author of numerous educational books. She is an avid football fan and spends many fall weekends watching college and NFL football.

PHOTO CREDITS